WITHDRAWN

# Space
# Adventure
# Crafts

Anna Llimós

**Enslow Elementary**
an imprint of

**Enslow Publishers, Inc.**
40 Industrial Road
Box 398
Berkeley Heights, NJ 07922
USA

http://www.enslow.com

# Con

Earth
page 4

Satellite
page 6

Martian
page 8

Sun
page 10

Rocket
page 12

Astronaut
page 16

# tents

**Astronaut Dog**
page 18

**Moon**
page 20

**Moon Fairy**
page 22

**Planets**
page 24

**Galaxy**
page 26

**Read About
and Index**
page 32

**Create Your Own Story**
page 28

**A Space Adventure**
page 30

# Earth

**1.** Cover the Styrofoam® ball with pieces of tissue paper. Coat the tissue paper with a glue wash. Let dry.

## Materials

- Styrofoam® ball
- tissue paper
- clay
- glue wash (1/2 white glue, 1/2 water)
- paintbrush
- dowel
- poster paint

**2.** Use clay to form the different continents.

**3.** Add a different color of clay to some of the continents.

**5.** Paint the dowel. Let it dry. Stick it into the meteorite. Stick the planet Earth onto the other end of the dowel.

**4.** Use clay to make a meteorite.

The bluest planet!

## Materials

* Styrofoam® ball
* paint
* marker
* 4 dowels
* clay
* white glue

**1.** Paint the ball. Let dry.

**2.** With the marker, draw a line around the ball. Draw some dots for the screws.

**3.** Paint the four dowels. Let dry.

**4.** Stick the four dowels into the ball.

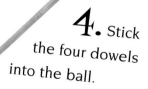

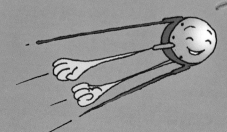

# Satellite

I'm happy!

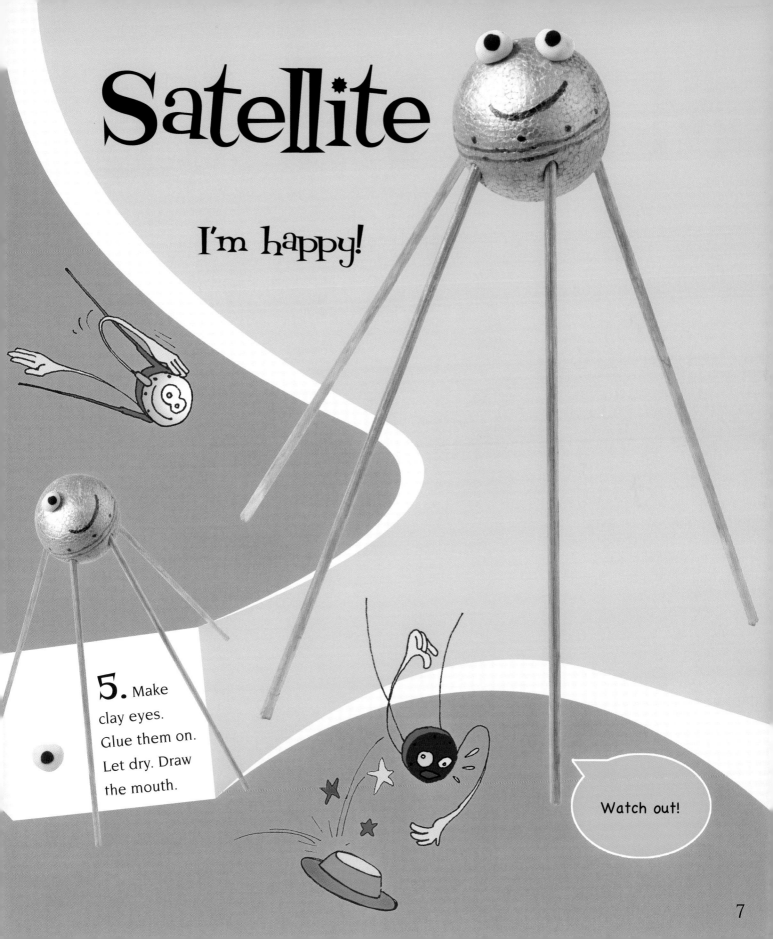

**5.** Make clay eyes. Glue them on. Let dry. Draw the mouth.

Watch out!

# Martian

## Materials

- empty yogurt container
- clay
- 2 paperclips, straightened
- toothpicks
- plastic knife

I'm on vacation!

**1.** Use clay to form the head, a trumpet-shaped nose, and the body. Attach the head to the body with a toothpick.

**2.** Make the eyes using two small pieces of clay. Draw the mouth with a toothpick.

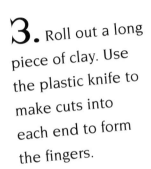

**3.** Roll out a long piece of clay. Use the plastic knife to make cuts into each end to form the fingers.

**4.** Attach the clay arms behind the Martian's head. Use two paper clips and two balls of clay to make the antennae.

**5.** Cover the edge of the yogurt container with clay and stick on little clay dots. Place the Martian inside of his flying saucer.

Watch out, everybody, here I come!

**1.** Cover the ball with clay, pressing down with your fingers.

**Materials**

* Styrofoam® ball
* toothpicks
* clay

I see something in the distance!

**2.** Stick in toothpicks of different lengths around the ball.

**3.** To make the sun's rays, cover the toothpicks with clay.

**4.** With a toothpick, draw the sun's smile.

# Sun

The brightest friend

**5.** Use clay to make the eyes.

# Rocket

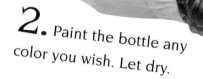

## Materials

* 1 plastic bottle
* newspaper
* white glue
* paintbrush
* cotton balls
* old toothbrush
  (Ask permission first!)
* poster paint
* clay
* toothpick
* markers

2. Paint the bottle any color you wish. Let dry.

1. Cover the outside of the bottle with newspaper dipped in glue. Let dry.

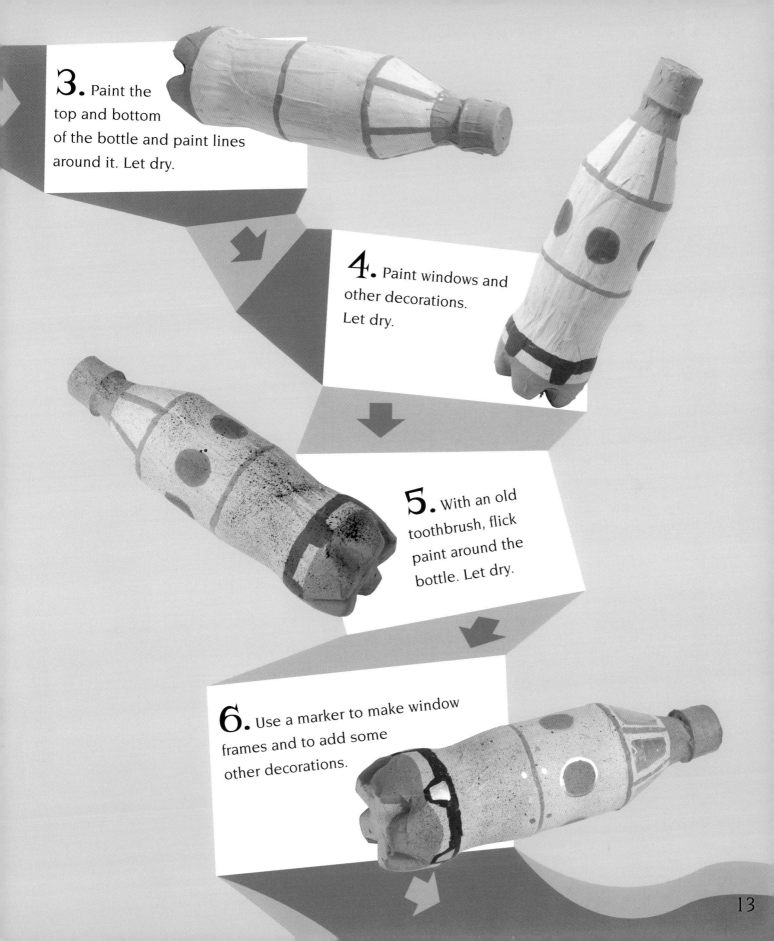

**3.** Paint the top and bottom of the bottle and paint lines around it. Let dry.

**4.** Paint windows and other decorations. Let dry.

**5.** With an old toothbrush, flick paint around the bottle. Let dry.

**6.** Use a marker to make window frames and to add some other decorations.

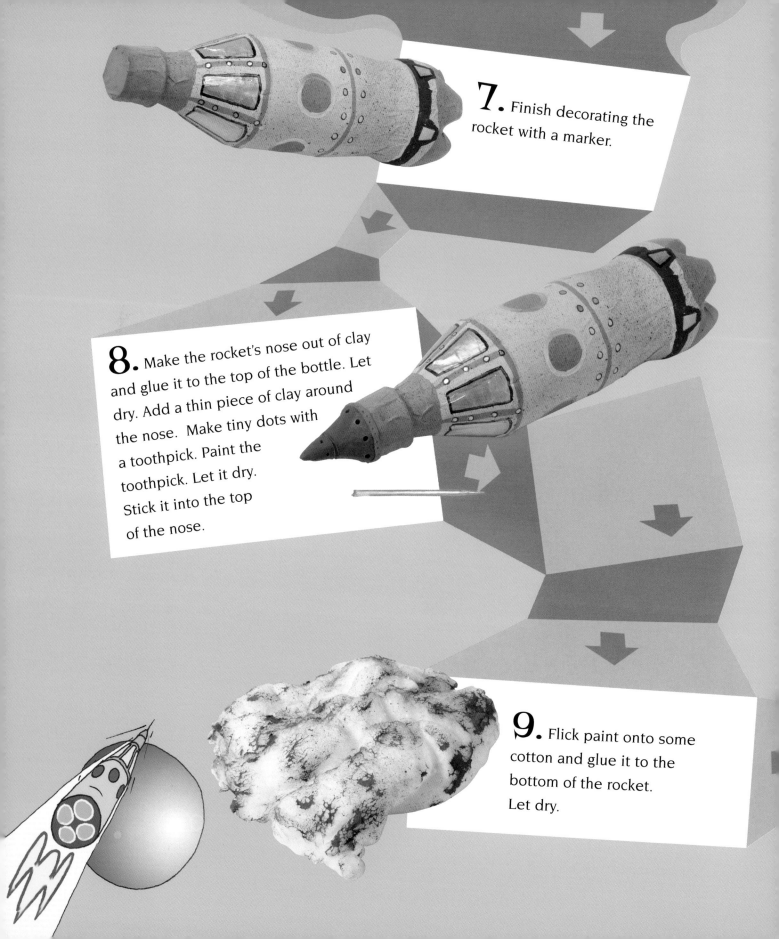

**7.** Finish decorating the rocket with a marker.

**8.** Make the rocket's nose out of clay and glue it to the top of the bottle. Let dry. Add a thin piece of clay around the nose. Make tiny dots with a toothpick. Paint the toothpick. Let it dry. Stick it into the top of the nose.

**9.** Flick paint onto some cotton and glue it to the bottom of the rocket. Let dry.

The rocket
is ready.

# Astronaut

I want
to go to
Mars!

## Materials

* craft foam
* colored tape
* marker
* scissors
* stapler
* white glue

**6.** To make the face, cut a circle out of craft foam. Make the eyes, nose, and mouth with a marker. Make a helmet from craft foam. Staple the head and the helmet together. Place the head in the groove above the arms.

**1.** Make a tube out of craft foam. Glue the edge and let dry. On one end of the tube, make two cuts for the legs. Make two smaller cuts into the other end of the tube.

**2.** Cut four strips from another piece of craft foam. Wrap them around the legs so there are two at the knees and two at the feet. Glue in place. Let dry.

No gravity!

**3.** Cut two more strips of craft foam and glue them on the feet. Let dry.

**5.** Cut two more strips of craft foam and stick them to the arms with colored tape. Stick pieces of colored tape onto the knees. Make a belt decorated with pieces of colored tape.

**4.** For the arms, cut a strip of craft foam and insert it across the two cuts at the top.

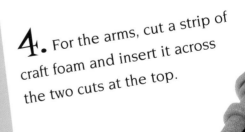

17

# Astronaut Dog

**Materials**
* clay
* toothpicks

Woof! What a spacesuit!

**5.** Use clay to make the dog's head. Make the nose and eyes out of small pieces of clay. Draw hair with a toothpick. Attach the head to the helmet with a toothpick.

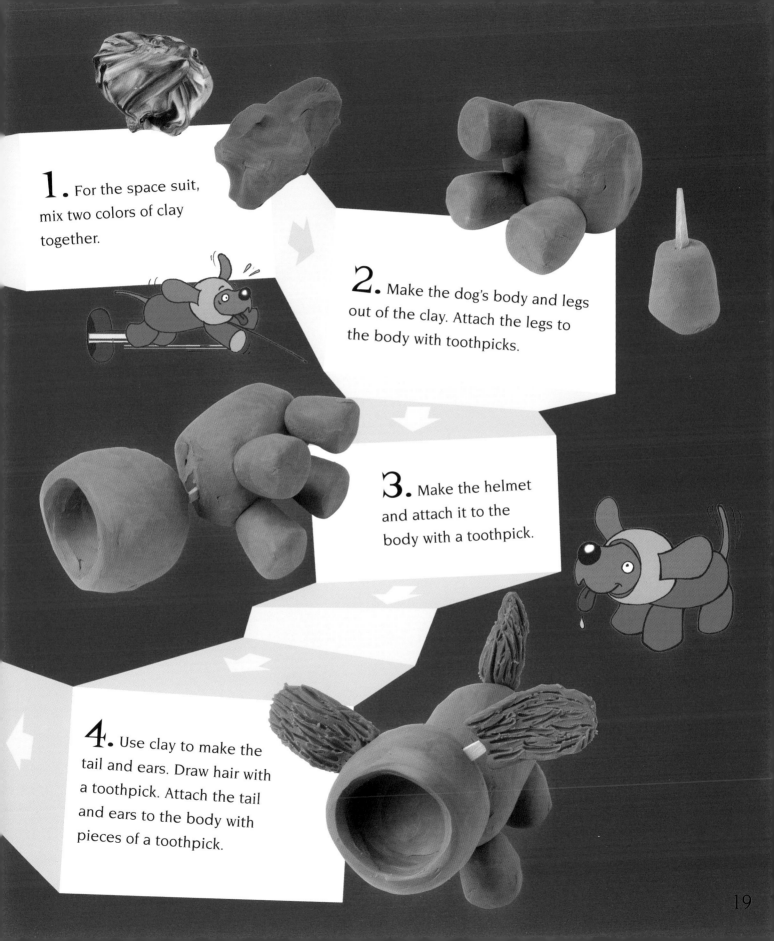

**1.** For the space suit, mix two colors of clay together.

**2.** Make the dog's body and legs out of the clay. Attach the legs to the body with toothpicks.

**3.** Make the helmet and attach it to the body with a toothpick.

**4.** Use clay to make the tail and ears. Draw hair with a toothpick. Attach the tail and ears to the body with pieces of a toothpick.

19

# Moon

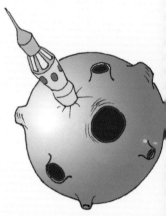

## What a bright moon!

**5.** Paint the moon and the insides of the craters. With the sponge, lightly paint some parts of the moon with different colors.

20

**1.** Draw a circle on the cardboard and cut it out.

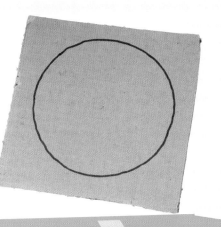

Woof! There is something in the crater!

**2.** Wrinkle some newspaper and place it on top of the circle. Secure it with masking tape. You will have half a sphere.

**3.** Cover the half sphere with pieces of newspaper dipped in white glue. Let dry.

**4.** Make craters of different sizes using clay.

## Materials

- clay
- egg carton cup
- aluminum foil
- toothpicks
- plastic knife
- poster paint
- old toothbrush (Ask permission first!)
- paintbrush

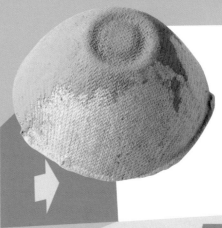

**1.** Cut out a cup from an egg carton and paint it. Let dry.

**2.** Use an old toothbrush to flick it with paint. Let dry.

**3.** For the arms, roll out a long piece of clay. Cut fingers into the ends with a plastic knife. Attach it to the body with a toothpick.

**4.** Mold the head out of clay with a cone at the top. Attach the head to the body with a toothpick.

# Moon Fairy

I live on the moon!

Please come again!

**5.** Attach clay eyes and a nose. Draw a smile with a toothpick. Wrap a strip of aluminum foil around the cone.

# Planets

**6.** You can make other planets of different sizes and colors and attach them to the meteorite.

Saturn, the ringed planet

**1.** For Saturn, make a ball out of clay.

**2.** On the cardboard, draw Saturn's rings and cut them out.

**3.** Paint the rings any colors you wish. Paint the dowel. Let them dry.

**4.** Attach the rings to the planet with a toothpick through each side.

**5.** Make a meteorite out of clay. Stick the dowel in it. Place Saturn onto the other end of the dowel.

## Materials

- thick cardboard
- poster paint
- scissors
- paintbrush
- old toothbrush (Ask permission first!)
- marker
- white glue
- stapler

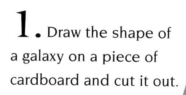

**1.** Draw the shape of a galaxy on a piece of cardboard and cut it out.

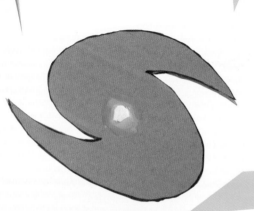

**2.** Paint the center and then paint around it in another color. Let dry.

**3.** Continue painting it with a darker color. Let dry.

**4.** Use an old toothbrush to flick paint on the galaxy. Let dry.

# Galaxy

A huge galaxy!

See you later!

**5.** For the support, fold a strip of cardboard into a triangle and staple the ends together. Glue it behind the galaxy. Let dry.

Create your own story with all the crafts in this book!

A Space Adventure

# On a very nearby moon . . .

The planets shine through the darkness of space. This is the blue planet, our Earth. A silver object flies from Earth!

It is the Satellite flying in space!
"Hello, Satellite, how are the pathways?"
"Be careful, it seems that there is a lot of traffic. There is danger of crashing."

"Watch where you're going!" a Martian yells. The Martian travels in his fast flying saucer. He takes a break from his long journey to say hello to a friend.

The brilliant Sun returns the greeting, and tells the Martian, "I have spotted something in the distance! It is a rocket that has blasted off from Earth."

"Hello, Satellite!"
"Hello, Rocket!"
Oh no, another collision in space! Earth, we have a problem!
They repair the rocket. We have made a perfect moon landing!

Our astronaut sets foot on the Moon. He floats like a feather because gravity is weaker. He lets his dog out of the rocket.

The dog looks around. The Moon looks like cheese with so many craters. The dog is very curious and finds a crater to explore.

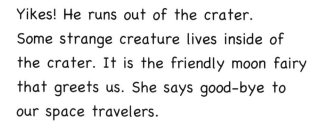

Yikes! He runs out of the crater. Some strange creature lives inside of the crater. It is the friendly moon fairy that greets us. She says good-bye to our space travelers.

They fly off for new adventures in space.

They cross the solar system to unknown galaxies. They discover constellations with a lot of light and colors. They wave goodbye and go off in search of black holes.

See you soon!

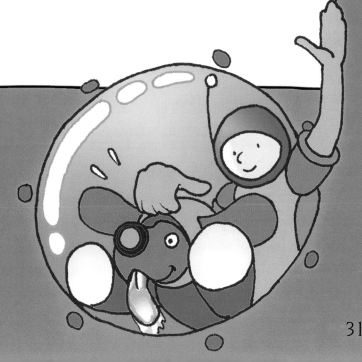

31

Enslow Elementary, an imprint of Enslow Publishers, Inc.
Enslow Elementary® is a registered trademark of Enslow Publishers, Inc.

English edition copyright © 2011 by Enslow Publishers, Inc.

All rights reserved.

No part of this book may be reproduced by any means without the written permission of the publisher.

Translated from the Spanish edition by Stacey Juana Pontoriero.
Edited and produced by Enslow Publishers, Inc.

**Library-in-Cataloging Publication Data**

Llimós Plomer, Anna.
[Crea tu. Odisea en el espacio. English]
Space adventure crafts / Anna Llimós.
p. cm. — (Fun adventure crafts)
Includes bibliographical references and index.
Summary: "Provides step-by-step instructions on how to make eleven simple space-themed crafts, such as a galaxy, rocket, Martian, and more, and it includes a story for kids to tell with their crafts"—Provided by publisher.
ISBN 978-0-7660-3732-8
1. Space flight—Juvenile literature. 2. Planets—Juvenile literature. 3. Handicraft—Juvenile literature. I. Title. II. Title: Odisea en el espacio.
TL793.L624 2010
745.5—dc22

2009041468
ISBN-13: 978-0-7660-3733-5 (paperback ed.)

Originally published in Spanish under the title *Crea tu . . . Odisea en el espacio*.
Copyright © 2009 PARRAMÓN EDICIONES, S.A., - World Rights.
Published by Parramón Ediciones, S.A., Barcelona, Spain.
Text and exercises: Anna Llimós
Illustrator: Àlex Sagarra
Photographs: Nos & Soto

Printed in Spain

122009 Gráficas 94 S.L., Barcelona, Spain

10 9 8 7 6 5 4 3 2 1

**To Our Readers:** We have done our best to make sure all Internet Addresses in this book were active and appropriate when we went to press. However, the author and the publishers have no control over and assume no liability for the material available on those Internet sites or on other Web sites they may link to. Any comments or suggestions can be sent by e-mail to comments@enslow.com or to the address on the back cover.

# Read About

## Books

Morris, Ting, and Neil Morris. *Space*. Mankato, Minn.: Sea to Sea Publications, 2007.

Sadler, Judy Ann. *The New Jumbo Book of Easy Crafts*. Toronto: Kids Can Press, 2009.

## Internet Addresses

**Crafts for Kids at Enchanted Learning**
<http://www.enchantedlearning.com/crafts/astronomy>

**Moon Rock Craft, DLTK's Crafts for Kids**
<http://www.dltk-kids.com/crafts/space/mmoon.html>

# Index

A Space Adventure
page 30

Astronaut
page 16

Astronaut Dog
page 18

Create Your Own Story
page 28

Earth
page 4

Galaxy
page 26

Martian
page 8

Moon
page 20

Moon Fairy
page 22

Planets
page 24

Rocket
page 12

Satellite
page 6

Sun
page 10